THE SECRET OF THE DECEIVING STRIPED LIZARD ... AND MORE!

BY ANA MARÍA RODRÍGUEZ

Enslow Publishing

101 W. 23rd Street
Suite 240
New York, NY 10011
USA

enslow.com

Acknowledgments
The author expresses her immense gratitude to all the scientists who
have contributed to the Animal Secrets Revealed! series. Their comments and
photos have been invaluable to the creation of these books.

Published in 2018 by Enslow Publishing, LLC.
101 W. 23rd Street, Suite 240, New York, NY 10011

Copyright © 2018 by Enslow Publishing, LLC.

Library of Congress Cataloging-in-Publication Data

Names: Rodriguez, Ana Maria, 1958- author.
Title: The secret of the deceiving striped lizard... and more! / Ana María
  Rodríguez.
Description: New York : Enslow Publishing, 2018. | Series: Animal secrets
  revealed! | Includes bibliographical references and index. | Audience:
  Grades 3 to 6.
Identifiers: LCCN 2017002984| ISBN 9780766086258 (library-bound) | ISBN
  9780766088535 (pbk.) | ISBN 9780766088474 (6-pack)
Subjects: LCSH: Protective coloration (Biology)—Juvenile literature. |
  Zoology—Research—Juvenile literature.
Classification: LCC QL767 .R63 2017 | DDC 591.47/2—dc23
LC record available at https://lccn.loc.gov/2017002984

Printed in the United States of America

To Our Readers: We have done our best to make sure all websites in this book were
active and appropriate when we went to press. However, the author and the publisher
have no control over and assume no liability for the material available on those websites or
on any websites they may link to. Any comments or suggestions can be sent by email to
customerservice@enslow.com.

Photo Credits: Cover Pan Xunbi/Shutterstock.com; pp. 3 (top left), 6 © Yuval Helfman/
Dreamstime.com; pp. 3 (top right), 17 © Sandyloxton/Dreamstime.com; pp. 3 (center left),
21 © Fimbriatus/Dreamstime.com; pp. 3 (bottom right), 27, 28, 29 Tobias Lortzing; pp. 3
(bottom left), 37 © Sergio Boccardo/Dreamstime.com; p. 7 © Xunbin Pan/Dreamstime.
com; p. 9 Gopal Murali; p. 11 © Pimmimemom/Dreamstime.com; p. 13 © Cathy Keifer/
Dreamstime.com; p. 15 (top) Pascal Damman; pp. 15 (bottom), 16 Fabian Brau; pp. 20,
22 Karen M. Warkentin; p. 23 Karen M. Warkentin and Marc A. Seid; p. 31 © Pipa100/
Dreamstime.com; p. 35 SeaPics; p. 36 Derke Snodgrass, NOAA/NMFS/SEFSC/SFD; p. 39
© Yuriy Ivanov/Dreamstime.com.

★ CONTENTS ★

★

ENTER THE WORLD OF ANIMAL SECRETS

In this volume of Animal Secrets Revealed!, you will meet the Indian scientist who designed a computer game to uncover the secret of striped lizards. Then, you will travel to Belgium and France, where physicists took on the challenge of measuring the sticky power of the chameleon's tongue. A trip to Panama will reveal the mystery of red-eyed tree frogs that hatch on cue. In Germany, you will meet biologists unraveling the old "friendship" between ants and the plant bittersweet nightshade. You will end your journey in the Netherlands with the scientists who uncovered that the swordfish head holds a secret of one of the fastest fish on Earth.

Welcome to the world of animal secrets!

4

1
THE SECRET OF THE DECEIVING STRIPED LIZARD

Gopal Murali, a computer scientist with a passion for reptiles, was spending an afternoon outdoors catching snakes. Suddenly, a snake with a bright, black-and-red-striped pattern caught his eye. Murali wanted to catch it. He had caught other snakes before. He didn't think catching the striped snake was going to be so difficult. He tried to grip the snake's body many times but missed. It seemed that his aim was always behind the snake, not on it. The striped snake got away.

Murali was frustrated but intrigued. He had been catching snakes and other reptiles since he was a child. Why was the striped snake so difficult to catch?

A snake with a red color and pattern similar to those of this garter snake inspired Gopal Murali to study striped lizards.

"I had to change my strategy to catch it," said Murali. He went back to the field and found the striped snake again.[1]

"This time, I concentrated on aiming ahead of the snake's path," said Murali. "It worked!"

Murali had succeeded at catching the striped snake, but he did not forget the experience. He was so curious about why striped snakes were so hard to catch that he did his doctorate project on this topic. He exchanged snakes for an easier subject, though. He studied striped lizards instead.

Wearing Stripes Is a Popular Style, for Lizards

Murali went to the library and studied books about lizards. He discovered that thousands of types of lizards, like many snakes, have striped, colorful patterns on their bodies. The stripes run along the lizard's body. Murali was surprised. The striped patterns seemed to do little to camouflage or allow the lizard to blend in with its surroundings. On the contrary, it seemed that the stripes made the lizards stand out. It would be easier for predators to see them.

The stripes along this blue-tailed lizard can confuse a predator and help the lizard escape capture.

In his readings, Murali learned that other scientists thought that the stripes on a running lizard create the illusion of the lizard moving slower than it really does. Murali wanted to test this idea.

Computer Games to the Rescue

At first, Murali thought about working with real animals outdoors to test the idea that stripes make lizards appear to be slower than they actually are. But the more he thought about it, the more he realized that he had to do it differently.

"I did not want to expose live lizards to real predators," said Murali. "Instead, I created a computer game."[2]

Murali had studied computer science in college. Thanks to that, he knew how to write a game people could

What Do Computer Scientists Do?
What Do Computer Scientists Do?
Computer scientists learn languages that computers use. Then, they write computer programs or instructions that tell computers what to do. Some programs instruct robots to move, speak, or play chess. Other computer programs help design animations, solve engineering problems (think of building a bridge), make your phone speak, create computer games, and many other activities to help people live better lives or just be entertained.

play on a computer. In the game, people played the role of predators. Their challenge was to "catch a lizard" that moved around the computer screen. The "lizard" was a black and white rectangle. To "catch it," players had to touch the screen. They would "catch" the lizard if they touched the front of the rectangle in the direction of movement. This would be like catching a real lizard by the head or the body. Touching the back of the rectangle would be like catching the lizard's tail. Then, in real life, the lizard would shake its body, break the expendable tail, and escape to a safe place.[3]

Some of the rectangles (lizards) in the game had stripes that covered half their length. Others had white splotches on a black background. The computer program counted automatically how many times players touched the screen. Murali then calculated how many of the hits had caught the head and how many the tail.

The Game Is On!

Murali was on a mission to find lizard hunters that would like to play his game. He talked to many of his friends and classmates. He explained that he needed only a few minutes of their time. All they had to do was play the game for one minute. They would play it once with striped lizards and another time with splotched lizards.

Murali asked other people to play a different type of game. In this game, players had to judge the speed of the "lizards" moving around on the computer screen. They had to decide whether the striped lizards were slower, faster, or equal in speed to splotched lizards.

Gopal Murali plays the lizard game on his computer.

Murali had no problem convincing people to play his games. They all enthusiastically agreed to help him with his project. In total, Murali got 240 people to play. Thanks to his friends, he collected enough data to answer his question.[4]

Before he had his results, Murali predicted in his hypothesis that if a striped pattern helped lizards escape more easily from predators, then computer game players trying to catch the lizards would have fewer hits on the head of the striped lizard and more on the tail. He also predicted that the number of hits in blotched lizard bodies and tails would be about the same.

Striped Lizards, Nature's Masters of Illusion

When Murali had the results of his experiment, he was delighted. Players had failed to catch the lizard more when it had a striped pattern than when it had a blotched pattern. The players who had to judge the lizard's speed thought that striped lizards moved slower than blotched lizards.

Murali put the two results together. The striped lizard is harder to catch than a blotched-patterned lizard most likely because the stripes in motion create the illusion that the lizard is moving slower than it actually is. The players miscalculated the lizard's speed and aimed short of the target. They did not get the head; they got the tail instead.[5]

> **What Is a Hypothesis?**
> A hypothesis is a prediction of the result of an experiment. If the result of the experiment matches the prediction, then the scientist most likely has an explanation for the phenomenon he or she is studying.

Stripes Make Lizards Safer in Plain Sight

Murali had uncovered the secret of the striped lizards. In the beginning, having a bright, colorful striped pattern on their

The colors and stripes of this six-lined racerunner whiptail provide camouflage in its environment.

bodies seemed to put lizards at a disadvantage. Predators would spot them easily because they stood out in their surroundings.

It turns out that it is true that wearing stripes makes lizards stand out. But stripes also create an illusion. Stripes trick the predator's mind into thinking that the lizards are moving slower that they actually are.

Wearing stripes allows lizards to be out and about in their environments looking for food or companions. They do not have to hide from predators as often because the stripes along their bodies make them less vulnerable to predator attacks. The predator miscalculates its aim, catches the expendable tail, and the lizard gets to live another day.

2
THE CHAMELEON'S STICKY TRICKS

A chameleon sits motionless on a tree branch; its body color blends in just right with the vegetation around it. It scopes its surroundings by turning its eyes in several directions without moving its head. It is looking for some-thing to eat—a cricket, perhaps. A lizard that is almost a third of the chameleon's size is close by. The chameleon, which is as large as a small cat, fixes its eyes on the lizard. In a fraction of a second, the cha-meleon shoots its long tongue out, captures the lizard, and pulls it back into its mouth.

This impressive feat would be like an 88-pound (40-kilogram) child catching a 26-pound (12-kilogram) turkey, a very large turkey, with his or her tongue! It is no surprise that scientists have been very curious about

A baby panther chameleon shoots out its tongue to catch a cricket.

what makes the chameleon's tongue so strong. The chameleon attracted the attention of physicists Pascal Damman, Fabian Brau, and Déborah Lanterbecq.

Powerful Muscles and Sticky Mucus

Scientists think that powerful muscles propel and retract the chameleon's tongue with millisecond speed. The tongue projects forward like the tubes of an extending telescope. It retracts like a spring.

Some scientists think that the tongue's grip power comes mostly from a suction-cup effect of the tongue's tip. However,

What Do Physicists Study?
Physicists study physics, a branch of science that deals with the physical characteristics or properties of matter and phenomena. For example, physicists study black holes, what makes planets orbit the sun, heat, light, sound, electricity, magnetism, gases, liquids, and solids and their properties, such as what makes them sticky.

Damman, Brau, and Lanterbecq were not convinced. They decided to study the chameleon's tongue from a physics point of view. They would bring new insights to better understand its powerful grip.

The tongue has a coat of mucus. Mucus is sticky, but how sticky is it? Nobody had measured the actual stickiness or viscosity of the mucus on the chameleon's tongue. The scientists took on the challenge.

Physics Meets Biology to Reveal the Secret of Mucus

"As physicists, we like to work together with biologists to study how living organisms work," said Damman, who is a professor at the University of Mons in Belgium. "But the methods we use in physics are very different from those biologists use."[1]

> ### Viscosity
> **Viscosity is a property of fluids—liquid-like substances—that helps them cling to a solid surface. For example, honey is more viscous, or "thicker," than water.**

Damman, Brau, and Lanterbecq first observed how chameleons catch their prey. Then, instead of doing experiments with chameleons as biologists would do, they built a simplified physical model to measure the viscosity of mucus. Using their measurement of mucus's viscosity, they then predicted the largest size of prey chameleons of different sizes would be able to catch. Finally, they met with biologists and compared the predictions with the

actual sizes of prey biologists
had found in chameleons'
stomachs.

**Pascal Damman's computer
screen shows an image of the
chameleon he studied.**

Beads and Mucus

Early one winter morning,
Brau and Lanterbecq jumped
in the car and drove to Pairi
Daiza, which is about thirty
minutes from the University
of Mons, where they work in Belgium. Pairi Daiza is a zoo and a
botanical garden that houses more than four thousand animals,
including chameleons. The zoo is not open to the public in winter. The scientists crossed a very lonely and quiet zoo as they
walked toward the building housing
the chameleons.

**Déborah Lanterbecq
places a small steel ball
on top of a glass slide as
Leïla-Nastasia Zghikh
observes.**

"I am used to going to the zoo
when it is full of people. It felt quiet,
nice, and strange during winter," said
Brau.[2]

In the building that housed the
chameleons, they met Vincent Bells,
a biologist who would help them get
mucus from chameleons. To collect
the mucus, the scientists tempted a
chameleon to shoot its tongue by

placing a cricket in front of it. They placed a microscope glass slide in front of the prey. When the chameleon shot its tongue, it struck the glass slide, leaving a coat of mucus.

Right away, the scientists rested the slide on an inclined surface, placed a small steel bead at the top of the slide, and let it roll. They filmed the bead rolling down the slide with a high-speed camera.[3]

The scientists repeated the experiment many times with three different chameleons. "When we were back at the university, we analyzed the movies to calculate the velocity or speed of the beads. From this velocity and other factors, we determined the viscosity of the mucus," said Brau.[4]

Fabian Brau analyzed the chameleon's data in his office.

After some mathematical calculations, they discovered that the chameleon's mucus is about four hundred times more viscous than human saliva. Then the scientists used the viscosity to predict the size of prey that chameleons of different sizes would be able to catch.

Chameleons, even those as small as this Southern dwarf chameleon, use the sticky power of their tongue to catch prey.

Their prediction was that if a chameleon with a size X is able to capture a prey of size Y, then a chameleon twice the size (2X) will be able to capture a prey with a size 2.5Y.

This result agrees with experimental data biologists provided. This made the researchers feel confident about their results. "I was delighted when I saw that our predictions matched the experimental data," said Brau.[5]

The three scientists and their colleagues had successfully used physics experiments and math to show the powerful grip of the mucus in the chameleon's tongue. They calculated that if the mucus were as sticky as human saliva, chameleons would

CHAMELEON FACTS

- **Most chameleons live in Africa and Madagascar; others live in Asia and Europe. They do not live naturally in the Americas.**
- **Chameleons come in a variety of sizes; some are as big as a small cat, and others can sit on the tip of a finger.**

be able to catch only prey that is roughly fifty times smaller than what they actually catch.[6]

The scientists think that the chameleon's tongue owes its power largely to the super sticky mucus. The tip of the tongue stretches over a large area of the prey, spreading the super sticky mucus. The mucus provides enough gripping power for chameleons to catch a large meal. This allows them to fill their stomachs with one large meal instead of having to hunt for several small meals.

3
THE SECRET OF THE QUICKLY HATCHING EGGS

It is warm and humid in the Smithsonian Tropical Research Institute in Gamboa, Panama. Kristina Cohen, a frog biologist, enters the air-conditioned laboratory. A friend turns on the music on her laptop. As the melody fills the room, Cohen sets up the video recording equipment. She is preparing for another all-night experiment making videos of frog eggs hatching.

Cohen studies the curious hatching strategies of the eggs of the colorful red-eyed tree frog. She wants to find out how the eggs hatch on cue. These experiments need Cohen to be very patient. She may need to repeat some of her tests several times until she gets good videos. The music was helpful. "We played silly music to keep us entertained," she said.[1] She and her friend sometimes sang along.

Kristina Cohen smiles at the Experimental Pond in Gamboa. Can you find the red-eyed tree frogs?

Several months later, Cohen asked her students to help her analyze the recordings. They watched the videos and suddenly started laughing. In the background of videos of frog embryos wriggling out of their eggs, they could hear Cohen's friend singing silly songs. Needless to say that the musical background did not make it to the videos' final cut.

Egg Surprise

The red-eyed tree frog lays eggs on plant leaves hanging above ponds. The frog sticks the eggs on the leaf with a transparent jelly, and then the frog leaves. The embryos inside the eggs are on their own. If nothing threatens their survival, they will hatch in six or seven days. Then, the little tadpoles will drop into the water and continue to grow and develop.[2]

If a snake or a wasp tries to eat the eggs before hatching time, the eggs will most likely hatch early. This is a very good strategy to avoid becoming a predator's meal. Scientists were surprised that red-eyed tree frogs and other animals could hatch on cue. Until recently, most scientists did not know that the frog embryos were capable of this feat.

Another surprise about these eggs is that they can hatch in a matter of seconds. The embryos inside the eggs can sense danger and respond quickly to escape death. This speedy reaction really works for the embryos. About eight of every ten embryos survive a life-threatening attack by quickly getting out of their eggs.[3]

Red-eyed tree frogs lay their eggs on leaves hanging over water.

Fascinated by the curious hatching strategies of the red-eyed tree frog, Cohen joined

> **Where Do Red-Eyed Tree Frogs Live?**
> Red-eyed tree frogs live in tropical areas in southern Mexico, throughout Central America, and in northern South America.

the lab of Dr. Karen Warkentin. She is a professor at Boston University and has been studying these frogs for years. Warkentin discovered that red-eyed tree frog embryos could hatch rapidly to escape from snakes and other predators.

Cohen decided to study how these eggs hatch so quickly. Nobody had explored this question before in these frogs. It turns out that she was the right person for the job.

"In my college ecology class, my professor took us to the woods and we learned about amphibians and their breeding," said Cohen. "I also did some research with fish in Trinidad. These experiences helped me know that I was interested in tropical biology. I like working with amphibians especially."[4]

When a cat-eyed snake attacks red-eyed tree frog eggs, the eggs hatch. Notice a newly hatched tadpole in mid-air.

Shake, Make a Hole, and Exit!

At first, Karen and her colleagues thought that the embryos made their way out of the eggs by wriggling and ripping the egg open. They had seen the embryos thrashing around inside the eggs, but nobody had studied in detail how the embryos actually set themselves free.

22

It all happened too quickly. They needed to see it in slow motion. A high-speed camera was the way to do it.[5]

At the Smithsonian Tropical Research Institute in Gamboa, Karen and her collaborator, Marc Seid, collected leaves with egg clutches from nearby ponds. They attached them to plastic cards and hung them over a container with water, to catch the tadpoles. They misted them often to prevent them from drying. They kept the egg clutches in an open-air laboratory, next to the air-conditioned lab where they did the video recordings.

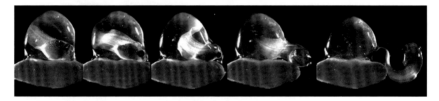

This sequence of still images from the high-speed video shows a red-eyed tree frog embryo hatching.

The scientists let the eggs develop for five days. Then, they gently removed single eggs, placed them individually on a platform, and started filming. Just moving the eggs to the filming location usually triggered hatching.

In the slow-motion videos, they discovered that most embryos shake lightly before hatching. They remain in one position inside the egg and open and close their mouths before the egg breaks open. Then, liquid inside the egg starts to leak where the embryo's snout meets the egg. The embryo plugs the hole with its snout and wriggles and thrashes to thrust its body through the hole.[6]

These observations revealed that the embryos did not just rip open the egg. Cohen suspected that the embryos first released some chemicals called enzymes from their snouts. These enzymes can make a hole in the egg. The embryo then pushed through this opening, thrashing until it was free.[7] To confirm this idea, Cohen took a closer look at the embryo's snout under an electron microscope.

Cohen had the idea, or hypothesis, that if the embryo used enzymes to make a hole in the egg, then the enzymes would be stored in vesicles or little sacs on the snout. These sacs would be full of enzymes before the embryos hatched, and mostly empty after the embryos had exited the egg.

> **The Electron Microscope**
> **The electron microscope is a type of microscope that allows scientists to magnify objects or see them much larger and in finer detail than a light microscope can. It uses a beam of electrons, instead of light, to create images. They are large, expensive machines.**

It took Cohen many attempts with the electron microscope to get a clear view of the embryo's snout. The efforts were worth the hard work. She confirmed her hypothesis. The embryos have hatching glands filled with egg-breaking enzymes concentrated on their snouts.

Cohen and her colleagues have uncovered the secret of the fast-hatching frog eggs. When a snake or a wasp threatens the eggs, they respond by speeding up the hatching process. The embryos pour enzymes from hatching glands on their snouts on a specific spot on the egg. The enzymes make a hole, the embryo quickly wiggles its way out, falls into the pond, and swims away from danger.

RED-EYED TREE FROG FACTS

- **Red-eyed tree frogs sleep during the day, hiding in the rainforest canopy—the maze of leaves and branches on treetops.**
- **At night, they catch crickets, flies, and moths with their long, sticky tongues.**
- **Their toe pads help them stick to surfaces and climb swiftly.**
- **They could easily fit in the palm of your hand. Adult males are about 2 inches (5 cm) long. The females are larger at 3 inches (7.5 cm).**

4
SWEETS AND ANTS PROTECT THIS PLANT

Anke Steppuhn, a plant ecologist, leaned closer to what was left of her bittersweet nightshade plants and frowned. Just overnight, the leaves were practically gone. The stems were chewed in so many places that they had fallen on the ground. Steppuhn and her doctorate student, Tobias Lortzing, had planted bittersweet nightshade in their garden at the Dahlem Center for Plant Science at Freie University of Berlin, Germany. They had planned to do experiments about a curious relationship between bittersweet nightshade and ants. But now they had no plants to work with.

"At first, we thought that somebody had destroyed our plants," said Steppuhn. "We planted more bittersweet and Lortzing put up signs asking people not to destroy the plants because we needed them to do our experiments."[1]

Next morning, the newly planted bitter-sweet nightshades lay on the ground, destroyed. "We were surprised it had happened a second time," said Steppuhn. "We had to solve this mystery before we could do our experiments."

Steppuhn and Lortzing woke up very early and headed toward the garden. They hoped they could catch the plant destroyer red-handed. When they reached the garden, they saw the plants lying on the ground again, but nobody was around. They got closer to the plants and

The team of scientists in the field look at the interactions between bittersweet nightshade plants, ants, and herbivores.

saw the culprits of the plants' demise. Slugs, some as big as a man's thumb, sat on the plant stems chewing out holes. Others were feasting on the leaves.

What Is Symbiosis?
Symbiosis is a relationship between two different organisms that benefits both.

27

The slugs are voracious herbivores—plant eaters—that feed only at night. "That's why we did not see them in the morning," said Steppuhn. She added jokingly, "The slugs had not read the sign about leaving our plants alone."[2]

The Mystery of the Sugary Droplets

Plants and ants have been helping each other for thousands of years. They are one of the most interesting examples of symbiosis in the natural world. Most ants do not chew on or eat plants. Actually, they usually protect them from herbivores such as the slugs that were destroying Steppuhn and Lortzing's garden.

However, in her garden, Steppuhn had seen ants that seemed to be chewing on wounds on leaves of bittersweet nightshade. "This is how this project started," said Steppuhn.

> **Leaf-Cutting Ants**
> Leaf-cutting ants are the only type of ants that cut plant leaves. Even in this case, the ants do not eat the leaves; they take them to their nest to grow a fungus, which is their main food.

This ant is consuming a sugary droplet from a leaf of bittersweet nightshade. It is a reward for defending the plant from herbivores.

"I wondered why these ants were different. Why were they attacking rather than helping these plants?"[3]

Steppuhn and Lortzing moved the plants into their greenhouse where it would be easier to study them. They observed that when herbivores such as slugs or beetles attacked the plants, especially the leaves, a clear liquid oozed out of the wounds. Plants with these droplets on the wounds had more ants on them than plants without them. The ants seemed to be feeding on the droplets. The scientists analyzed the droplets and discovered that they were mostly sugar.[4]

A close-up photograph show the sugary droplets oozing from a leaf of bittersweet nightshade.

It made sense that the sugary droplets were attracting the ants because ants like sugar. However, Steppuhn and Lortzing had to prove it with experiments. In the greenhouse, they set up two separate groups of bittersweet nightshade plants. On one group, they applied sugary droplets they had prepared mimicking the ones oozing from wounds caused by herbivores. On the second group of plants, they applied sugarless water droplets.[5]

VERY OLD FRIENDS

That ants can defend plants that produce sugary droplets or nectar is not a new idea. However, until Steppuhn, Lortzing, and their colleagues worked with bittersweet nightshade plants, scientists thought that plants made nectar only with special structures called nectaries. Nectaries are in the flowers and can be in other parts of the plant. Bittersweet nightshade plants, on the other hand, do not have nectaries. What is new about this work is that we now know that plants do not need nectaries to produce nectar.[6] This work hints that plants and ants most likely have been able to team up to help each other survive for much longer than we thought before. They did not have to wait for nectaries to evolve. They are very old friends indeed.

The scientists allowed slugs and beetles to have access to both groups of plants. After a few days, the scientists counted how many ants were on the plants with sugary droplets. They compared this number with that of the plants with sugarless droplets. They also determined the number of holes herbivores chewed on the leaves.

Steppuhn, Lortzing, and their colleagues were excited about the results. The plants with sugary droplets attracted more ants than those with sugarless droplets and were half as damaged by herbivores.

Ant Bodyguards

How do ants manage to reduce herbivore damage to the plants? This was a bit of a mystery, too. Were the ants attacking the slugs directly or discouraging them from feeding on the plants another way?

Steppuhn and Lortzing arranged another set of experiments to answer this question. They had two groups of plants. Both groups were available to slugs, but ants visited only one group. After a few days, the scientists checked on the plants and the slugs. The plants that ants visited had less damage to the leaves and more dead slugs than the plants without ants. In addition, the slugs that had survived ant attacks did not grow to be as large as slugs not exposed to the attacks. The ant bodyguards aggressively attacked and killed slugs that wanted to feed on bittersweet nightshade plants.[7]

Bittersweet nightshade has green and red berries and purple flowers. You can find this vinelike plant throughout the United States, Canada, and parts of Europe and Asia. The leaves and berries are poisonous.

There was still another mystery. Beetles made more wounds on the plants than slugs did. However, the ants did not attack the beetles as they did the slugs. In the case of the beetles, both adults and larvae feed on the plants.

To solve this riddle, the scientists carried out another experiment. They compared the fate of beetles and their larvae in the presence and in the absence of ants. The ants spared the adult beetles, but they carried the larvae to their nest. This prevented the larvae from chewing on the new plant shoots. When ants are around, the plants have fewer larvae and grow more than when ants are absent.

Steppuhn, Lortzing, and their colleagues have uncovered the secret of how ants and bittersweet nightshade plants help each other better survive in their environment. When wounded by herbivores chewing on their leaves and stems, the plants ooze sugary droplets that attract ants. The ants feed on the droplets, and in return for the easy meal, they aggressively defend the plants by killing the herbivores.

Science Tongue Twisters
- **The scientific name of bittersweet nightshade plants is *Solanum dulcamara*.**
- **The slug's name is *Arion vulgaris-rufus-ater*.**
- **The beetle's name is *Psylliodes dulcamarae*.**
- **The name of the ants that helped bittersweet nightshade plants the most is *Myrmica rubra*.**

5
SLICK AND FAST

It is 2 a.m. John Videler and Ben Szabo sneak quietly through a back door of the Academic Hospital at Groningen in the Netherlands. They are pulling a heavy gurney—a stretcher on wheels—covered with a green sheet. Inside the hospital, a few volunteer staff members are waiting to help them carry a very unusual "patient" to the MRI machine.

The "patient" is a dead swordfish. Videler is a scientist. Szabo is the head of the radiology department in the hospital. He had offered to make MRI scans of the swordfish at night, when there were no real patients scheduled to use the machine. These would be the first MRI scans ever made of a swordfish. The scans would let the scientists see what the insides of the swordfish look like.

"We put the thawed swordfish in the MRI machine and scanned the entire fish," said Videler. "When we finished, we sprayed the room with forest-scented spray to try to disguise the fishy smell."[1]

> ### What IS an MRI Machine?
> **MRI, or magnetic resonance imaging, is a test to make pictures of the organs inside the body. The MRI machine makes those pictures with magnetic fields and radio waves. In comparison, an X-ray machine makes pictures of the inside of the body with X-rays.**

Big and Fast

Videler has been studying fish for more than forty years. He was curious about what makes swordfish one of the fastest fish in the ocean. Swordfish bodies can be as heavy as a large jet ski, nearly 1,200 pounds (540 kilograms). Many weigh about half that weight. The largest swordfish can be as long as a basketball hoop is high above the court. That is about ten feet (three meters).

Despite being so large, a swordfish can zoom at 62 miles (100 kilometers) per hour. It could rush past an Olympic swimmer in a flash but would be head-to-head with a jet ski speeding at top regulation speed (65 miles per hour, or 105 kilometers per hour).

The swordfish's streamlined figure helps it swim fast.

Swordfish are made to swim fast. They have a strong, smooth-shaped body and scaleless skin and fins. Videler was impressed by the swordfish's long, flat, rough, and sharp bill. It seems the fish can swing its bill right and left to strike or slash prey before swallowing it with its toothless mouth. Scientists know this because they have studied what is inside the swordfish's stomach. They have found squid and fish with marks similar to cuts.

The bill's slick design also helps swordfish swim fast. The bill's shape reduces the amount of drag pulling the fish back as it speeds through the water. Videler and Szabo suspected that swordfish had more secrets about what makes them one of the fastest animals in the water. They hoped the MRI scans would help clarify the mystery.[2]

Taking a Fishy Gift Home
One of the hardest things for Videler was to get hold of a swordfish to study. He lives in the Netherlands, bordering the

35

North Sea. Swordfish roam most of the oceans, but not the North Sea.

"Luckily, I had been teaching a course in marine biology in Corsica, a French island in the Mediterranean Sea where swordfish live," said Videler.[3]

During his visits to Corsica, Videler made friends with fishermen and told them about his passion for swordfish. Next thing, the fishermen gave

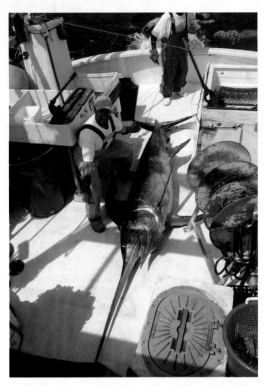

A fisherman is amazed at the size of the swordfish he caught.

Videler two whole swordfish. The fish were 5.2 feet (1.6 meters) long, about as tall as most women in the United States are. The fishermen had bent the fish to fit them inside their freezer. Videler had to thaw the swordfish, straighten them, and freeze them again before wrapping them between mattresses for the flight back home.

Somehow, Videler managed to take the frozen swordfish back to his laboratory in the Netherlands. He slid the swordfish on gurneys past customs officials without being asked any questions. He rented a car and rode to his lab at Groningen

University with the swordfish still frozen. He stored them in a long freezer he had bought especially for the fish.

Days later, Videler and Szabo were sneaking into the MRI facility.

Looking Closer Inside the Swordfish Head

MRI scans and other studies have revealed some of the swordfish's secrets. For starters, Videler and his colleagues discovered a gland inside the swordfish's head, just where the bill enters the skull. The gland takes up about half of the space in that part of the head. Nobody had seen this gland before.[4] The gland is full

The oil gland is inside the swordfish's skull, where the bill joins the head.

SWORDFISH FACTS

- Swordfish migrate through most of the oceans on both sides of the equator, eating a variety of fish and squid. They avoid cooler waters nearer to the poles.
- Female swordfish are larger than males.
- Swordfish are a blackish-brown color above that fades to a lighter shade below. The fins are brown.
- Killer whales are one of the few predators of adult swordfish. Sharks and other large fish prey on young swordfish.

What Is a Gland?
A gland is an organ that makes a particular substance for the body to use. For example, the pancreas is a gland that makes insulin, a hormone that helps the human body use sugar. Sweat glands make the sweat that cools the body.

of oil. The scientists wondered what the oil is for. The answer to the mystery of the oil gland had to wait a little longer.

Years after Videler had studied the first MRIs of the swordfish head, Roelant Snoek, a student in Videler's lab, took on the challenge of uncovering the secret of the oil gland. He wanted to find out whether there was a connection between the nostrils—the openings at the end of the nose—and the oil gland. The secret, however, proved hard to crack. After half a year of hard work, Snoek was not able to solve the mystery; he found no connection with the olfactory system. He was about to give up. Videler told him that he had done an excellent job. Some secrets are hard to uncover.

Sailfish, which can swim as fast as swordfish, are part of big-game fishing.

"Before he left, I asked Snoek to take a few additional photographs of the olfactory organ, the swordfish nose," said Videler.[5]

"A True Light Bulb Moment"

Snoek was setting up his photographic equipment to take the pictures Videler had requested. He was about to place a bright light above the animal's head when the light slipped from his hands and fell on top of the fish's head. And then, he saw them. The light shone through the skin, revealing a network of very thin tubes—capillaries—running from the gland to the surface of the skin.

Snoek was very excited! He decided to extend his time in Videler's lab. His studies revealed that when heated, the capillaries ooze the oil onto the skin through tiny pores, or holes.[6]

Videler, Snoek, and their colleagues have uncovered another secret of one of the fastest fish on Earth. The scientists think that the oozing oil makes the swordfish head slippery. As the fish darts through the ocean, the slippery head reduces the drag slowing the fish down. The swordfish speeds up, quickly slashing at a squad of squid. Dinner is served!

> **Science Tongue Twisters:**
> **The swordfish's scientific name is _Xiphias gladius_. _Gladius_ means "sword" in Latin.**

HANDS-ON ACTIVITY

Sticky Race

Many animals and plants use sticky substances. People, for instance have sticky mucus inside the nose. It helps trap airborne microbes that could enter the body and make a person sick. Saliva is also sticky. Chameleons have mucus that is many times as sticky as human saliva. Scientists call sticky substances viscous. The more viscous a substance is the more it sticks to surfaces.

In this experiment, you will compare the viscosity of several substances.

What you need:
- ★ A cookie pan
- ★ A white piece of paper that fits the backside of the pan
- ★ Plastic wrap
- ★ Tape
- ★ Pencil
- ★ Ruler
- ★ Modeling clay
- ★ Water
- ★ Oil
- ★ Honey
- ★ Liquid hand soap
- ★ Paper towels
- ★ Five stopwatches
- ★ A box about 4 inches (10 cm) high
- ★ A team of six people

What to do:
1. Draw a line on one end of the paper. Label it "Start."
2. Draw another line on the opposite end. Label it "Finishing Line."

3. Draw four equally distant lines between the start and the finish line. Make five lanes for a race.
4. Cover the backside of the pan with the paper. Secure it with tape.
5. Cover the white paper with plastic wrap. Secure it with tape.
6. Make five small clay balls, each about 0.4 inches (1 cm) wide.
7. Lay the pan flat on a table. Place the finish line on top of paper towels.
8. Pour two tablespoons of the substances (water, oil, honey, liquid hand soap) each on a lane at the start. Leave one lane without a substance.
9. Carefully, place a clay ball on each lane.
10. Ask each member of your team to get ready to start his or her stopwatch.
11. Slowly, incline the start side of the pan and lift it onto the box.
12. As you incline the pan, ask your team to start their stopwatches.
13. Each team member will stop the stopwatch when the ball he or she is watching reaches the finish line.
14. Repeat the experiment one more time. Before the race, predict in which order the balls will reach the finish line.

Substance	First race (min)	Second race (min)	Average (min)
None			
Water			
Honey			
Liquid hand soap			
Oil			

Results

1. Copy the table onto a piece of paper. Record your results.

2. Calculate the average of the two races for each substance.

$$\text{Average} = \frac{(\text{minutes in race 1}) + (\text{minutes in race 2})}{2}$$

3. Display your results in a bar graph.

4. How do your results compare to your predictions?

5. Order the substances from least viscous to most viscous.

6. Try other substances in the race.

★ CHAPTER NOTES ★

Chapter 1: The Secret of the Deceiving Striped Lizard

1. Dr. Gopal Murali, Skype interview with author, October 6, 2016.
2. Ibid.
3. Gopal Murali and U. Kodandaramaiah, "Deceived by Stripes: Conspicuous Patterning on Vital Anterior Body Parts Can Redirect Predatory Strikes to Expendable Posterior Organs," *Royal Society Open Science*, vol. 3:160057 (June 8, 2016), doi: 10.1098/rsos.160057.
4. Dr. Murali.
5. Murali and Kodandaramaiah.

Chapter 2: The Chameleon's Sticky Tricks

1. Dr. Pascal Damman, email interview with author, October 19, 2016.
2. Dr. Fabian Brau, email interview with author, December 12, 2016.
3. Fabian Brau, Déborah Lanterbecq, Leïla-Nastasia Zghikh, Vincent Bels, and Pascal Damman, "Dynamics of Prey Prehension by Chameleons Through Viscous Adhesion," *Nature Physics*, vol. 12 (June 20, 2016), p. 931, doi:10.1038/nphys3795.
4. Dr. Brau.
5. Ibid.
6. Brau, et al.

Chapter 3: The Secret of the Quickly Hatching Eggs

1. Dr. Kristina Cohen, email interview with author, October 19, 2016.
2. Kristina Cohen, M. A. Seid, and K. M. Warkentin. "How Embryos Escape from Danger: The Mechanisms of Rapid Plastic Hatching in Red-eyed Treefrogs," *Journal of Experimental Biology*, vol. 219 (2016), p. 1875, doi:10.1242/jeb.139519.
3. Ibid.
4. Dr. Cohen.

5. Ibid.

6. Ibid.

7. Ibid.

Chapter 4: Sweets and Ants Protect This Plant

1. Dr. Anke Steppuhn, Skype interview with author, October 12, 2016.

2. Ibid.

3. Ibid.

4. Tobias Lortzing, O. W. Calf, M. Böhlke, J. Schwachtje, J. Kopka, D. Geuß, S. Kosanke, N. M. van Dam, and A. Steppuhn, "Extrafloral Nectar Secretion from Wounds of *Solanum dulcamara*," *Nature Plants*, vol. 2 (2016), 16056.

5. Dr. Tobias Lortzing, email interview with author, December 13, 2016.

6. Lortzing, et al.

7. Ibid.

Chapter 5: Slick and Fast

1. Dr. John J. Videler, email interview with author, October 6, 2016.

2. Ibid.

3. Ibid.

4. John J. Videler, D. Haydar, R. Snoek, H. J. Hoving, and B. G. Szabo, "Lubricating the Swordfish Head," *Journal of Experimental Biology*, vol. 219 (2016), p. 1953.

5. Dr. Videler.

6. Videler, et al.

★ GLOSSARY ★

camouflage ★ Body colors and patterns that help an animal blend in with its environment.

deceive ★ To give a mistaken impression.

electron microscope ★ A type of microscope that uses a beam of electrons to create larger images of very small objects.

enzyme ★ A type of protein that can digest certain materials.

gland ★ An organ in the body that produces chemical substances that help the body work.

greenhouse ★ A glass building to grow plants.

hatch ★ To exit an egg.

herbivore ★ An animal that eats only plants.

larva ★ An immature animal that will develop into an adult.

MRI ★ Magnetic resonance imaging, done by machines that use electromagnetic radiation to make images of soft tissues inside the body.

mucus ★ A slimy substance.

olfactory system ★ A group of organs used for smelling.

predator ★ An animal that hunts and eats other animals.

prey ★ An animal hunted by other animals.

slug ★ A soft, slimy, wormlike animal.

symbiosis ★ A close association between particular plants or animals that usually benefits both.

vesicle ★ A small sac in the body that is usually filled with liquid.

viscous ★ Thick and sticky.

voracious ★ Very hungry.

★ FURTHER READING ★

Books

Carson, Mary Kay. *How Strong Is an Ant?: And Other Questions about Bugs and Insects.* New York, NY: Sterling Children's Books, 2014.

Mattison, Chris. *Chameleons.* Richmond Hill, ON, Canada: Firefly Books, 2012.

O'Shea, Mark. *Exploring Nature: Incredible Lizards.* Helotes, TX: Armadillo Publishing, 2013.

Simon, Seymour. *Frogs.* New York, NY: HarperCollins, 2015.

Websites

Smithsonian's National Museum of Natural History

youtube.com/watch?v=Q_D2ZMqmgMQ

Watch a video with fascinating facts about swordfish.

Warkentin Lab

sites.bu.edu/warkentinlab/video-library

Watch videos of red-eyed tree frog embryos hatching.

★ INDEX ★